COMPUTER-FREE CODING

GET CODING WITH DATA

What types
of data are there
and how do you
use them?
Find out with fun
puzzles and games!

Kevin Wood

WINDMILL BOOKS™

New York

Published in 2018 by **Windmill Books**, An Imprint of Rosen Publishing
29 East 21st Street, New York, NY 10010

Produced for Windmill Books by Alix Wood Books
Designed by Alix Wood
Editor: Eloise Macgregor
Editor for Gareth Stevens: Kerri O'Donnell

Photo credits: Cover background © Shutterstock; All robot artwork © Adobe Stock Images and Alix Wood;
all other art © Alix Wood

CATALOGING-IN-PUBLICATION DATA

Names: Wood, Kevin.
Title: Get coding with data / Kevin Wood.
Description: New York : Windmill Books, 2018. | Series: Computer-free coding | Includes index.
Identifiers: ISBN 9781499482560 (pbk.) | ISBN 9781499482539 (library bound) |
    ISBN 9781499482454 (6 pack)
Subjects: LCSH: Computer programming--Juvenile literature. | Algorithms--Juvenile literature. |
    Computer science--Mathematics--Juvenile literature.
Classification: LCC QA76.6 W66 2018 | DDC 005.1--dc23

Printed in the United States of America
CPSIA compliance information: Batch # BS17WM: For further information contact Gareth Stevens, New York, New York at 1-800-542-2595.

Contents

Coding and Data

Computers are very obedient. They will do exactly what you tell them to do. The instructions you give them are written in code. All kinds of household things have computers in them, and their coding tells them what to do. Cell phones, washing machines, and even some toys use code — in fact, just about everything powered by electricity uses code!

WHAT IS DATA?

Computer data is information **processed** or stored by a computer. Data could contain all different kinds of information. It could be words, images, numbers, or sounds. Data has to be organized in a special way so that the computer can understand it.

...“Add Two”

ERROR!

When you write code it is important to tell the computer what **data type** to expect. That way the computer will be able to process it correctly. If your code is expecting numbers, and you tell it to add “two,” instead of “2,” your code will not work.

Computers use a special type of **logic** known as **binary**. Binary logic uses two electrical states — on or off. Any data a computer uses has to be converted into binary. The binary number system uses two numbers — 0 and 1. 0 = off, and 1 = on.

1 0 0 1 0 0 0

Why is it called binary?

The "bi-" in binary means "two." "Bi-" is used in several words to do with the number two. "Bicycle" means two wheels.

GET Programming

It is important to give your computer very clear instructions. Computers can't guess what you mean. The instructions below are meant to tell a computer how to make toast, but they are all scrambled. Can you sort them into the correct order?

a) Put slice of bread in toaster

d) Spread butter on toast

b) Put toast on plate

e) Take slice of bread out of package

c) Wait until toast pops up out of toaster

Answers are on page 32

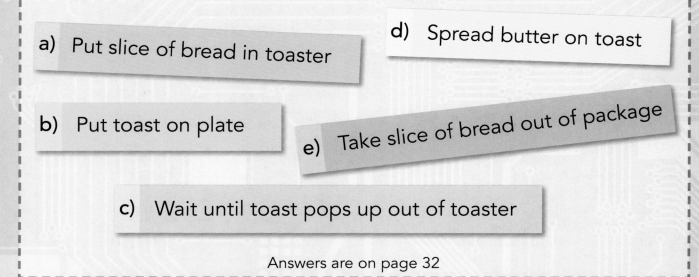

Types of Numbers

Numbers are just numbers, right? Not when you are coding. Numbers can be **integers**. Integers are whole numbers, such as 1, or 27. Numbers can also be **floating-point numbers**. Floating-point numbers are not whole numbers. They can be written as a fraction such as 1½, or as a decimal such as 1.5. In coding, they are written using a **decimal point**.

Why should we care about the types of numbers?

Because you need to decide which type of number you are expecting when you write your code.

Integers are whole numbers. Integers can be **positive** whole numbers, such as 12. They can also be **negative** whole numbers, such as -12. Zero is also an integer.

Which of these is a whole number, or integer?

Answers are on page 32

Coders need different types of numbers because integers and floating-point numbers behave in different ways. If you wanted to write a **program** that added together how many cell phones a family had, the program would only need integers.

2 (mom and dad's phones)
+ 1 (oldest child's phone)
+ 1 (youngest child's phone)
= 4 phones

If you needed to add the height of several people together, in feet, your operation would need to use floating-point numbers.

5.5 feet + 4.8 feet = 10.3 feet
(1.7 m + 1.5 m = 3.2 m)

Why not always use floating-point numbers?

Adding integers is faster and uses less **memory** than adding longer floating-point numbers.

GET Programming

Work out the answers to the puzzles below. Will your code need to use integers or floating-point numbers?

1. How many girls in a family?
Number of people in family = 5
Number of boys in family = 2

Subtract the number of boys from the number of people in the family.
Is your answer
a) an integer
b) a floating-point number?

2. Sharing the cookies
The number of cookies = 7
The number of people = 2

Divide the number of cookies by the number of people.
Is your answer
a) an integer
b) a floating-point number?

Answers are on page 32

All About Integers

Can you think of a program you might want to write that will only need integers? Most code only uses integers. You may want your program to do something a certain number of times, or draw an object to a certain width.

MEMORY

An integer is stored using one or more bits. A bit is the smallest unit of information stored in a computer's memory. As computers use a number system that only uses 0 and 1, each bit can have a value of either 0 or 1. As you add bits, the largest value you can have will increase.

How many bits would I need to work with 8 numbers?

You would need 3 bits. Each bit you add stores 2 times more information than the previous bit.

Remember 0 is a number

1 bit 1 x 2 = 2	0 and 1
2 bits 2 x 2 = 4	0,1,2,3
3 bits 4 x 2 = 8	0–7
4 bits 8 x 2 = 16	0–15

Coders only use as many bits as their data will need. The more bits coders give to an integer, the higher its largest value can be.

NEGATIVE INTEGERS

A negative number is a number with a minus sign in front. Say you want to write a program that counts down the seconds until recess. You will need to count down -1 from each second until the correct time, so your code will need to use negative numbers. Integers that may need to be negative are known as **signed integers** or "int." Integers that won't ever use a minus sign are known as **unsigned integers** or "uint."

CODING TIPS

Using unsigned integers means the numbers can be twice the value of signed integers. That is because signed integers have to fit positive and negative numbers in the same memory space.

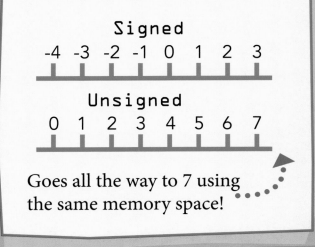

Goes all the way to 7 using the same memory space!

GET Programming

When people write code they often use shortened words. It's faster than typing out whole words. Coders use "int" for signed integers and "uint" for unsigned integers. They often use "_" as a space between words, too. Can you work out the code below and see which answer best matches the questions?

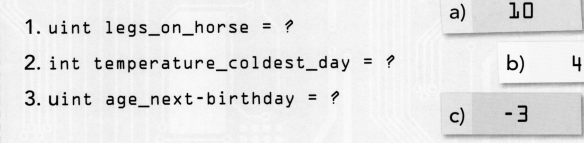

1. `uint legs_on_horse = ?`

2. `int temperature_coldest_day = ?`

3. `uint age_next-birthday = ?`

a) 10

b) 4

c) -3

Answers are on page 32

Understanding Floats

Floating-point numbers are sometimes called real numbers, or "floats" for short. The decimal point in a float may move around depending on how the number needs to be used. That is why it is described as floating. Coders normally use floats when they need to play with decimal numbers, such as in programs involving money or math.

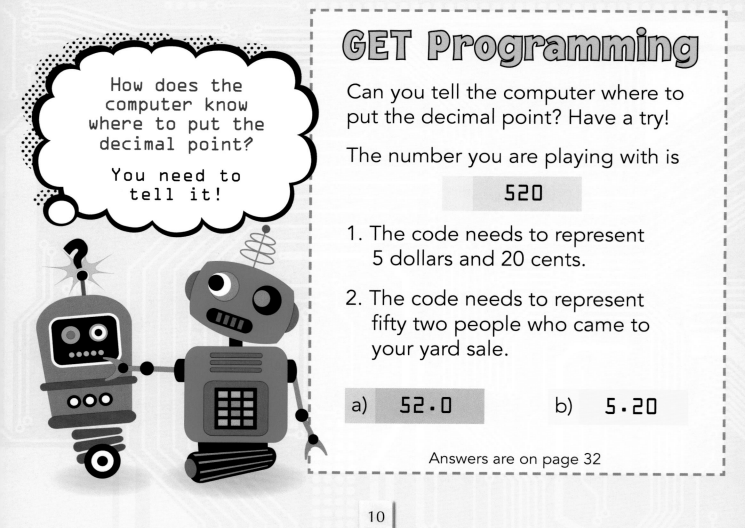

How does the computer know where to put the decimal point?

You need to tell it!

GET Programming

Can you tell the computer where to put the decimal point? Have a try!

The number you are playing with is

520

1. The code needs to represent 5 dollars and 20 cents.

2. The code needs to represent fifty two people who came to your yard sale.

a) 52.0

b) 5.20

Answers are on page 32

CODING TIPS

Programs written to expect an integer that are given a float instead will ignore, or round up or down, any number after the decimal point.

ROUNDING UP AND ROUNDING DOWN

Imagine that big robots are represented as a whole number and little robots are a half (0.5). You have to write some code to give everyone an airplane seat. Your total comes to 4.5. The code might round up to 5, or round down to 4. The little robot will either get his own seat, or have to sit on a big robot's lap! Sometimes writing code that recognizes floats is important.

1   2   3   4   .5

INTEGER OR FLOATING-POINT CHALLENGE?

See if you can work out if people will give you an integer or a floating-point number when they answer these questions.

1. How many legs does your pet have?

2. How much of the pizza did you eat?

3. What page of this book are you reading?

4. How much of this book have you read?

Answers are on page 32

Logic Data

In the 1800s, a man named George Boole developed a great system that all computers use today. He didn't develop it for computers because they didn't exist then. Early computer developers realized Boole's system was perfect, because it simply asked whether something was true or false. For a device that only uses 0 and 1, this was perfect.

TRUE OR FALSE?

When you write code you ask questions. A **Boolean** data type has only two possible values — true or false. For this reason it is sometimes called a Yes/No data type.

TRUE

FALSE

BOOLEAN CHALLENGE

Imagine you are a computer. If a statement is true, you must stand up. If it is false, sit down.

1. The robot on the left is orange.
2. The moon is square-shaped.
3. Ducks have three legs.
4. 3 is less than 5.
5. Dogs go "Baa."

Did you go up, down, down, up, down? If you did, you got it right!

GET Programming

When planning how to write code, programmers will often draw a flowchart. The chart gives you a chance to think through your code in a logical way. Try this fun flowchart. Simply answer yes or no and find out if you are actually a donkey!

Are you a donkey?

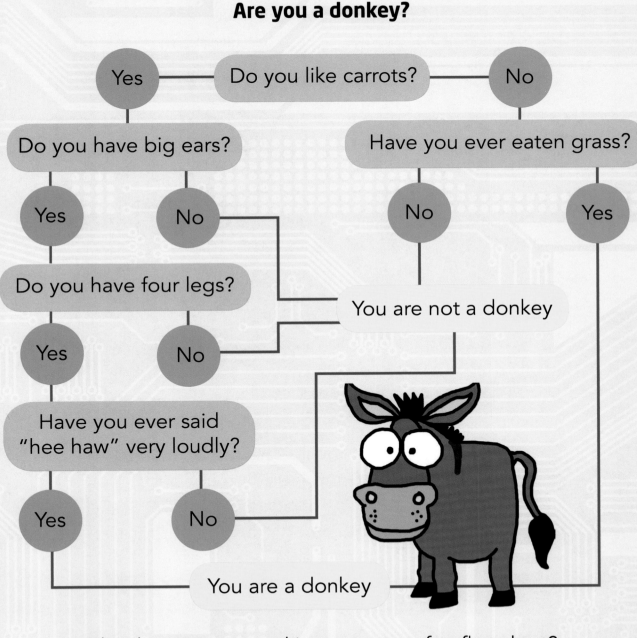

Yes — Do you like carrots? — No

Do you have big ears?

Have you ever eaten grass?

Yes / No

No / Yes

Do you have four legs?

You are not a donkey

Yes / No

Have you ever said "hee haw" very loudly?

Yes / No

You are a donkey

Why don't you try making your own fun flowchart?

Characters

How does a computer deal with an alphabet? A computer uses a data type known as "characters". A character is a unit of information, usually a symbol, such as a letter of the alphabet, or a punctuation mark. Can you imagine how you get a computer to know all the different characters a keyboard can make? The answer is back to simply 0 and 1!

THE ANSWER IS ASCII

When you write a message on your computer and send it to someone, how does their computer know what you typed? Coders use ASCII. Each letter and symbol is given a number. That number is then translated into a 7-bit binary number, made up of 0s and 1s. 127 possible characters can be given a code in this way.

If you look at the chart on page 15, you'll see that the letter A has an ASCII code of 65. Read the numbers on the top line of this chart from right to left. You'll see each number is twice as big as the one before. That's how binary works.

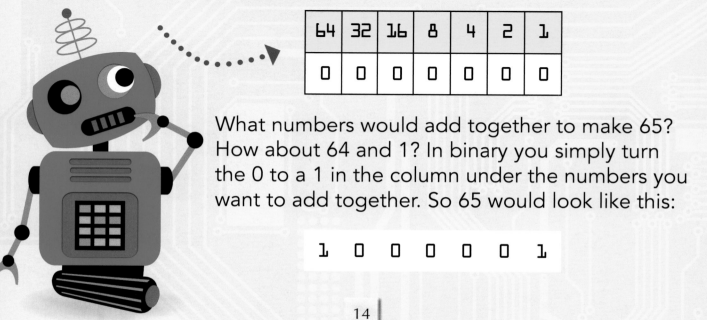

64	32	16	8	4	2	1
0	0	0	0	0	0	0

What numbers would add together to make 65? How about 64 and 1? In binary you simply turn the 0 to a 1 in the column under the numbers you want to add together. So 65 would look like this:

1	0	0	0	0	0	1

GET Programming

ASCII	Letter
65	A
66	B
67	C
68	D
69	E
70	F
71	G
72	H
73	I
74	J
75	K
76	L
77	M
78	N
79	O
80	P
81	Q
82	R
83	S
84	T
85	U
86	V
87	W
88	X
89	Y
90	Z

The table on the left shows you the ASCII numbers given to all the uppercase (A) letters of the alphabet, Lowercase (a) letters have different numbers.

Get a pen and paper and jot down the table below to help you. You can write your 0s and 1s underneath as you go along.

64	32	16	8	4	2	1

Work out what this coded message says. Find the letter that each binary code stands for by adding together the numbers in columns where any 1's appear. Write down each letter in order and the message will appear!

1	0	0	1	0	0	0
1	0	0	0	1	0	1
1	0	0	1	1	0	0
1	0	0	1	1	0	0
1	0	0	1	1	1	1

Answers are on page 32

What does ASCII stand for?

It stands for American Standard Code for Information Interchange. You can see why they shortened it!

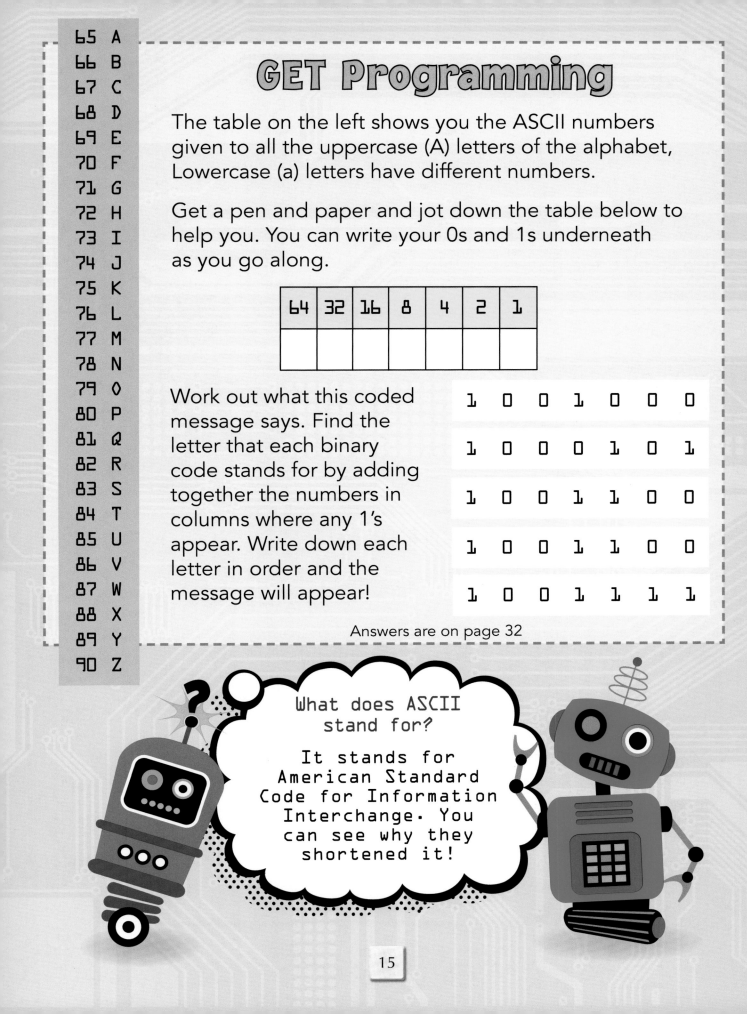

Strings

Characters that are joined together to form words are called **strings**. Strings are such an important kind of data they are used in nearly every programming language. Every word that you type on a keyboard is a character string.

"STRING"

Strings are usually written enclosed in quotation marks, like this — "String." The quotation marks tell the computer to recognize the data as a string rather than any other data type.

SPOT THE INVISIBLE!

The number of characters a string contains is called its length. "Party" for example, is five characters long. Not all characters you use on a keyboard are visible, though. Can you think of any keys that you type that don't produce a letter, a number, or a symbol? Even though you can't see the character, it still counts as part of the string's length.

This string has 10 characters. What key did we press to make the invisible character?

"Good Night"

Answers are on page 32

There is a big difference between how computer code will treat an integer and how it will treat a string. Strings are no use when it comes to math. If you ask the computer to add the string "two" to the string "three" the answer you would get would be:

"twothree"

That won't help you with your homework!

> Joining two strings together so they become one is known as **concatenation**. "Hello World"

CODING TIPS

When writing code, the multiplication sign is typed "*," instead of "x." This is so it doesn't get confused with the letter x.

GET Programming

Which of these pieces of code would actually get you the math answer to the question "What's 4 multiplied by 2?"

a) `"four" * "two"`

b) `4 x 2`

c) `"four" * 2`

d) `4 * 2`

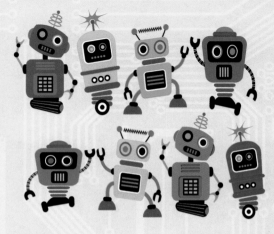

Answers are on page 32

Constants

Data that will never change are known as **constants**. For instance, the number of seconds in a minute is a constant. A minute will always be 60 seconds. A constant in code has a name, and a value. The name explains what the constant is. In this case the value is 60.

Constants are useful. Say we got our value wrong, and there were really 59 seconds in a minute. That's obviously not true, but let's imagine! Instead of changing the value everywhere it appears in our code, we just have to change the constant once, and the new value will appear everywhere it is used!

If a constant never changes, how did you change it?

It never changes while the program is running. You can change a constant once the program stops.

READABLE CODE

One of the best things about constants is that they make your code more readable. Sometimes code can be a baffling list of numbers and commands, and you can't remember what they all were and what you were intending them to do! Because constants describe what they are, you can scan back through your code and make sense of it more easily.

CODING TIPS

Is your code WET or DRY? DRY stands for "Don't Repeat Yourself." Good code is as short as it can be, easy to understand, and doesn't repeat itself.

WET stands for "Write Everything Twice", "We Enjoy Typing," or "Wastes Everyone's Time!" because long, muddled code is hard to read!

GET Programming

Imagine you want to program some friends to jump.
You could either:
a) go to each one and say "Jump 3 times" or
b) you could write "Jump 3 times" on a blackboard.

Which method would be better if you needed to change your value?
What about if you had 40 friends?

Writing the value on the blackboard means you could change your instruction to be "jump the number of times written on the blackboard."

3

Variables

Data that may need to change is known as a **variable**. Just like a constant, a variable has both a name and a value. The value can change while the program is running. There are lots of times you might want to use a variable when you code.

A variable is a little like a box. You can store data in it. Then you can use the information in your box for later use. Each variable is given a name. When you type the variable's name into your code it will go get the thing that you put in that box.

GET Programming

When you play a computer game, your score is stored as a variable. Each time you get a point, the variable will add 1 to your score total.

Get a box and "program" it to be a variable by writing "+1" on the side of the box. Now play this game. Try to throw some scrunched-up balls of paper into the box. Your box will keep score! Each time you hit, your variable goes up by 1. If you miss, your total stays the same.

CODING TIPS

A variable's value doesn't have to be a number. It can be a string too. For instance, your code could ask for a **User**'s name. What the User then types in is a variable. You can't predict what they will type. Call your variable UserName. You can now call up the User's name any time you need it by typing:

```
print (UserName)
```

Are variables stored on a computer?

No, they are usually temporary unless you save them.

SILLY SENTENCES

Try this variable sentence maker. Get four boxes to hold your variables, a pen and some paper. Label the boxes "family," "actions," "adjectives," and "animals." Write down the following words on the paper:

six family members	such as sister, brother, granddad
six actions	such as tickled, sniffed, jumped on
six adjectives	such as spotty, wobbly, crazy
six animals	such as elephant, mouse, piglet

Put each word in the correct variable box. Run your code:
Say "My <FAMILY> <ACTIONS> the <ADJECTIVES> <ANIMAL>"

Pick one variable from each box.
Read your sentence aloud!
"My sister sniffed the spotty piglet"

Random Numbers

Sometimes when coders are writing computer games they might want the computer to pick a random number. A random number is a number chosen at random, so it is impossible to predict what it will be. When coding games, programmers might use random numbers if dice are rolled or playing cards are dealt.

CAN COMPUTERS REALLY BE RANDOM?

No, even the most powerful computer can't actually create a truly random number. Computers are calculating machines. Random numbers can't be the result of a calculation. You might be able to predict the outcome if you knew how the calculation was done.

So, how does a computer create a random number?

Coders create a math formula so complicated that we just can't work out the pattern.

CODING TIPS

It's quite difficult to invent a random number generator. If you want a shortcut, though, programming languages already have built-in random number generators. So just use theirs!

It takes a lot of complicated code to get a computer to produce a random number. First, the computer needs a number to start the calculation with, known as a **seed**. It might use the number of milliseconds from when the computer was started, as that can seem like a random number. The result of each random number generation becomes the seed for the next one. It gets very complicated!

Random numbers in code are often called pseudo-random numbers. "Pseudo" comes from the Greek word meaning "false."

GET Programming

You can make your own truly random number generator though, with two boxes and some pieces of paper. To get a random number from 0–99, you will need to put the numbers 0–9 on scraps of paper into two boxes.

Mix the paper around a little and then shut your eyes and draw out one piece of paper from each box. Lay the numbers on the ground and there you have your random number! You can do something a computer can't do!

Using Arrays

When writing code you often have to store lists of things. Instead of making a variable for each item, you can store them in an **array**. An array is like a box with many compartments. Everything in the box has something in common. It may be a list of towns, or things you need to take on vacation.

PLAYING WITH LISTS

Each item in a list is known as an **element**. You can add or take away elements any time. Once you have made your list, you can easily refer to anything in it in your code. First, give your array a name. Let's call ours "Robot_Friends." Then write your list giving each friend a number:

Robot_Friends (1) = Bloop
Robot_Friends (2) = Sleebot
Robot_Friends (3) = Zarkle
Robot_Friends (4) = Churtle

Now you can call up each individual robot friend by their number.

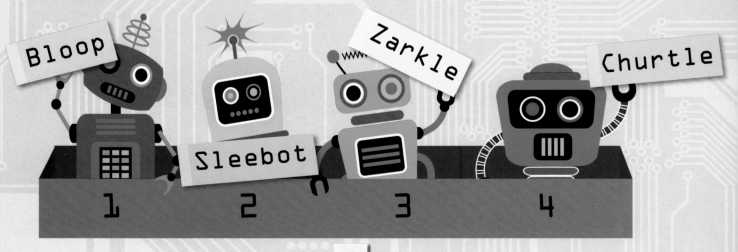

Arrays allow several related values to be kept in one place. All the data in an array must be the same data type. The robots' names in the array on page 24 are all strings. If you wanted to also store the year each robot was built, you would have to have another array which accepted just integers. These multi-arrays that give information about the same thing are common in programming.

CODING TIPS

You can place and sort elements in an array in a number of ways. You can place and retrieve an element in any order (random). You can also choose to use them in "First In First Out" order, known as FIFO. Or you can use them in "Last In First Out" order, known as LIFO.

GET Programming

LIFO or FIFO? Different situations require different ways of using arrays. Imagine you were making a stack of pancakes. You are most likely to want to sort that array as Last In First Out, because it would be easiest to take the last pancake from the top than one in the middle or bottom of the pile. If you were working at a store checkout, you would want to sort people in line in a First In First Out order.

Look at the situations below. Can you decide which order you would prefer to use them in; random, LIFO or FIFO?

1. A stack of magazines
2. Milk cartons in the refrigerator
3. Chocolates in a selection box
4. A line of traffic at a stop sign

Answers are on page 32

Making Images

Coders use data to create images. Images are made up using tiny blocks known as **pixels**. Images are measured by how many pixels they have, and their color depth. Pixels is short for "picture elements." Screens are also measured in pixels and in dpi, or dots per inch. If your screen is 72 dpi, that means that every 1-inch (3 cm) square is made up of a grid 72 pixels high by 72 pixels wide. The higher the dpi, the sharper an image looks.

I can't see any tiny blocks on my screen. Are you sure?

Yes, every screen displays images using pixels. Try zooming in really close and you'll see them!

BLACK, WHITE, AND RAINBOW COLORS

Each color used in an image is stored as a binary number. In a black-and-white image, each pixel is either black or white. The color data is quite simple, you give a value of 0 for white and 1 for black, so you only need to give each pixel one bit of memory. The more bits you assign to a pixel the more colors it can be. Most computers use 24-bit images, with over 16 million possible colors per pixel!

GET Programming

Take a sheet of squared paper and draw a grid of 8 rows by 11 columns like the one pictured below. Each square represents a pixel. Each line of binary 1-8 equals one row on your square. Moving along each row, color squares with a 1 black. Leave squares with a 0 white. We have done the first row for you.

Can you guess what the picture will be?

Answers are on page 32

Row 1: 1, 0, 0, 0, 0, 1, 0, 0, 0, 0, 1

Row 2: 1, 0, 0, 0, 0, 1, 0, 0, 0, 0, 1

Row 3: 0, 1, 0, 0, 0, 1, 0, 0, 0, 1, 0

Row 4: 0, 1, 0, 0, 1, 1, 1, 0, 0, 1, 0

Row 5: 0, 0, 1, 0, 1, 0, 1, 0, 1, 0, 0

Row 6: 0, 0, 1, 0, 1, 0, 1, 0, 1, 0, 0

Row 7: 0, 0, 1, 1, 0, 0, 0, 1, 1, 0, 0

Row 8: 0, 0, 0, 1, 0, 0, 0, 1, 0, 0, 0

Using more small pixels makes an image look smoother than using fewer large pixels.

DESIGN YOUR OWN

Try to design your own binary picture using squared paper. Then write out your instructions and challenge a friend to draw your image. Were your instructions clear? Did they get it right?

Can You Pass the Test?

1. What two numbers does binary use?
   a) 0 and 1 b) 1 and 2 c) 0 and 2

2. Which of these is a floating-point number?
   a) 5 b) 0 c) 2.7

3. Is zero an integer?
   a) yes b) no

4. What is "-25"?
   a) an unsigned integer b) a signed integer

5. A Boolean data type only has two possible values — true or false. Is this statement
   a) true b) false

6. How do you write the letter "A" in binary? Its ASCII number is 65.
   a) 0100001 b) 1000001 c) 65

7. Which of these is a string?
   a) 4 b) P c) robot

8. How many characters does this string have?
   "Red Robot"
   a) 8 b) 9

I think I got some right! Did you?

9. What does DRY stand for?

10. Should this data be a constant or a variable?
A circle is 360 degrees.
a) constant b) variable

11. Your pet hen lays 1 egg a day.
Should you use your eggs in
a) LIFO order b) FIFO order?

12. What is a pixel?
a) a tiny block on a computer screen
b) a robot

13. Which of these pieces of code might need a random number?
a) some code to display today's date
b) some code in a game that gives you the result of a dice throw

Turn this page upside-down to see the answers.

Quiz Answers

1. a) 0 and 1; 2. c) 2.7; 3. a) yes; 4. b) a signed integer 5. a) true 6. b) 1000001; 7. c) robot; 8. b) 9; 9. Don't Repeat Yourself; 10. a) constant; 11. b) FIFO; 12. a) a tiny block on a computer screen; 13. b) the dice throw

Glossary

array A group of mathematical elements.

binary A system of numbers having two as its base.

Boolean A system of symbolic logic devised by George Boole; used in computers.

concatenation To link together in a series or chain.

constants A quantity whose value does not change.

data type A particular kind of data item.

decimal point The dot at the left of a decimal (.678) or between the decimal and whole number (3.678).

element A single part of a larger group.

floating-point numbers Numbers which contain a decimal point that can float.

integers A whole number.

logic Sound reasoning.

memory The capacity for storing information.

negative Less than zero.

pixels Any of the small elements that together make up an image.

positive A number greater than zero.

processed To take in and organize for use in a variety of ways.

program Step-by-step instructions that tell a computer to do something with data.

seed The starting value used by a random number generation routine to create random numbers.

signed integers A whole number that may use a minus sign.

strings Sequences of characters such as numbers and letters.

user The person who operates a computer.

unsigned integers A whole number that will not use a minus sign.

variable A quantity that may take on any one of a set of values.

BOOKS

Rusk, Natalie. *The Scratch Coding Cards: Creative Coding Activities for Kids.* San Francisco, CA: No Starch Press, 2017.

Woodcock, Jon. *Coding Games with Scratch.* DK Children, 2015.

For web resources related to the subject of this book, go to: **www.windmillbooks.com/ weblinks** and select this book's title.

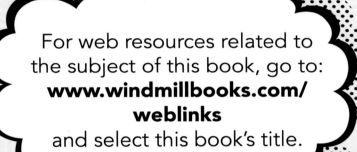

Index

Answers

page 5: e) Take slice of bread out of package, a) Put slice of bread in toaster c) Wait until toast pops up out of toaster b) Put toast on plate, d) Spread butter on toast; page 6: -4; page 7: 1 a, 2 b; page 9: 1 b, 2 c, 3 a; page 10: 1 b, 2 a; page 11: 1 integer, 2 floating-point number, 3 integer, 4 floating-point number; page 15: HELLO; page 16: the space bar; page 17: d; page 25: 1 LIFO, 2 FIFO, 3 random, 4. FIFO; page 27: W